Masks

Emma Lewis

Photography by Lyz Turner-Clark

CELEBRATION PRESS

Pearson Learning Group

Clean up!

When you see the words *Clean up!*, this means clean up any mess you have created. When you finish making your masks, put away all your equipment and materials.

Contents

Marvellous Masks

Masks are a lot of fun at a party, a school play, or just for dressing up on a rainy day. The masks in this book are made from paper plates, plastic cups, and different kinds of paper. Follow the designs in this book or try making up your own.

These pages list all the equipment and materials you will need to create your mask collection.

Equipment

- scissors
- adhesive tape
- pencil
- glue
- hole punch

Materials

- paper plates
- elastic string
- plastic cups
- colored and black paper
- colored tissue paper

Basics for All Masks

For each mask you make, you will need eyeholes. You will also need to attach elastic so that you can wear the mask.

Making the Eyeholes

1 Hold the plate to your face and mark on the plate where your eyes are. These marks will show you where to cut the eyeholes.

2 Draw circles for the eyes on your paper plate.

3 Cut out the eyeholes.

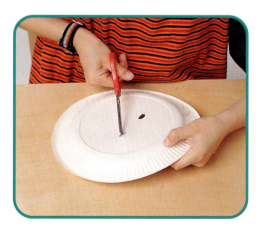

Attaching the Elastic

1 First, punch a hole with the hole punch on each side of the plate.

2 Cut a length of elastic long enough to go around the back of your head, from one ear to the other.

3 Push one end of the elastic through one hole and tie a knot. Push the other end of the elastic through the other hole and tie a knot. The elastic is now attached.

Would you like to be a red-eyed frog? A lion? Pick a mask from the next few pages and get started! With each mask plan, you will find a list of everything you need to create that particular design.

Red-Eyed Frog Mask

Equipment and Materials

To make a red-eyed frog mask, you will need the equipment shown on pages 4 and 5. You will also need a paper plate, black paper, red tissue paper, dark green and light green tissue paper, two plastic cups, and elastic.

Getting Started

When you have collected your materials and equipment, turn to pages 6 and 7. Follow the instructions to make the eyeholes and attach the elastic. Then continue with the instructions on page 9.

The Red-Eyed Frog Takes Shape

1 Tear up pieces of dark and light green tissue paper.

2 Glue pieces of dark green tissue paper all over the top half of the plate and light green tissue paper all over the bottom half. Be careful not to cover the eyeholes.

3 Use scrunched-up dark green tissue paper to make the frog's mouth. Carefully glue it to the plate between the dark and light green sections.

4 Using the base of a plastic cup, draw two half-circles at the top of the plate. This is where you will stick on the frog's eyes.

5 Cut out the two half-circles.

6 To make the eyes, cut off two-thirds of the plastic cups.

7 Cover each cup base with red tissue paper. Then cut out two diamond shapes from the black paper. Glue on the diamonds to complete the eyes.

8 Turn the mask over. Tape the eyes into the half-circle spaces.

9 Allow 10 minutes for the glue to dry and then try on your mask!

Clean up!

Leo the Lion Mask

Equipment and Materials

To make a Leo the Lion mask, you will need the equipment shown on pages 4 and 5. You will also need a paper plate, light and dark brown paper (crepe and tissue), black and light grey paper, and elastic.

Getting Started

When you have collected your materials and equipment, turn to pages 6 and 7. Follow the instructions to make the eyeholes and attach the elastic. Then continue with the instructions on page 13.

Leo the Lion Takes Shape

1 Tear up pieces of light brown and dark brown tissue paper. Glue them all over the plate. Be careful not to cover the eyeholes.

2 Cut out strips of dark brown and light brown crepe paper to make a mane.

3 Glue the strips of dark brown and light brown crepe paper all the way around the edge of the paper plate.

4 To make the lion's eyes, draw two large leaf shapes on the black paper. Then draw circles inside the leaf shapes. These circles should be the same size as the eyeholes on your plate.

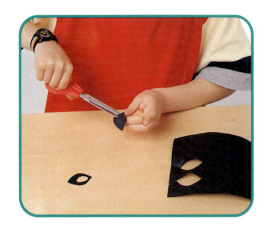

5 Cut out the two leaf shapes. Then cut out the inner circles.

6 Glue the eye shapes over the eyeholes on the mask.

7 To make the lion's nose, draw a triangle on the black paper.

8 Cut out the triangle. Glue it on the mask.

9 To make the lion's mouth, draw a moustache shape on the black paper.

10 Cut out the moustache shape. Glue it on the mask.

11 To make the lion's whiskers, cut out thin strips of light grey paper. Glue them on the mask.

12 Allow 10 minutes for the glue to dry and then try on your mask!

Ideas for Other Masks

What other masks can you make?

Ollie Owl

Fifi Fish

Patsy Parrot

Polka Polar Bear